Denial

*A Quick Look of History of Comfort Women
and Present Days' Complication*

Pacific Atrocities Education

Denial

*A Quick Look of History of Comfort Women
and Present Days' Complication*

Sophia Maroulis

Denial

*A Quick Look of History of Comfort Women
and Present Days' Complication*

Written by
Sophia Maroulis

Editor
Stacey Anne Baterina Salinas

Copy Editor
Martin Mayhew

Published by Pacific Atrocities Education

Paperback ISBN: 978-1-947766-48-8
E-book ISBN: 978-1-947766-47-1

Table of Contents

Introduction

No. 9 Army Film & Photographic Unit, Titmuss A D (Sergeant). Post-Work: User: W.wolny. *Chinese girl from one of the Japanese Army's 'comfort battalions,'* 8 August 1945.[1]

---

1. Photograph. Photograph SE 4523 from the collections of the Imperial War Museums. Source: Wikimedia Commons. https://commons.wikimedia.org/w/index.php?title=File:Chinese_girl_from_one_of_the_Japanese_Army%27s_%27comfort_battalions%27.jpg

"Comfort women" is the euphemism Japanese soldiers used to describe the approximately 200,000 women and girls the Imperial Japanese Army (IJA) forced into military-sponsored sexual slavery in the 1930s and throughout World War II.[2] Recent scholarship and human rights organizations that focus on the discussion of "comfort" argue that the phrase minimizes the violence that sexually enslaved people experienced while the use of the word "women" hides the fact that many of these "comfort women" were minors between the ages of 13 to 17. Many scholars now agree that "military sex slaves" is the most accurate term.

The term "comfort women" persists, however, many historians differentiate this uniquely large-scale and military-organized system of sexual exploitation from other forms of human trafficking. The IJA took an estimated 80% of the 200,000 women and girls from Korea, and the remaining 20% from other occupied parts of Asia such as China, the Philippines, Indonesia, Taiwan, and Burma.[3] Due to the percentage of Korean comfort women and the greater number of class-action lawsuits by former Korean comfort women, the scope of this work focuses primarily on Korean comfort women. Further scholarship and activism need to be done to tell the stories of comfort women from other countries. Recently, historians have estimated that both the number of total comfort women and the number of Chinese

2. Chunghee Sarah Soh. "Japan's National/Asian Women's Fund for 'Comfort Women,'" *Pacific Affairs* 76, no. 2 (2003), 1227.

3. Ibid.

comfort women are even higher. The vast majority of comfort women were taken from Korea, both because Japan colonized Korea from 1910-1945 and because Japan did not interpret trafficking people from its colonies as being in violation of the 1921 League of Nations treaty against international human trafficking.[4] Most comfort women were recruited under false pretenses for job offers in waitressing, housekeeping, and nursing; many were taken by coercive measures, and still more were abducted in broad daylight. Comfort women were held against their will and raped by Japanese soldiers in military brothels called "comfort stations."

Additionally, most of these women suffered beatings, torture, forced pregnancies, forced abortions, forced sterilizations, and medical complications from terrible living standards and from contracting venereal diseases. Many comfort women were victims of femicide. Throughout World War II, many comfort women died alongside IJA soldiers from the bombing of Allied powers. After the war, only an estimated 25% of comfort women survived and they faced great stigma as survivors of sexual violence.[5] Women discovered to be former comfort women were often disowned by their

4. Yuki Tanaka, *Japan's Comfort Women: Sexual Slavery and Prostitution During World War II and the US Occupation.* London: Taylor & Francis Group, 2001, 26; Pyong Gap Min, "Korean 'Comfort Women': The Intersection of Colonial Power, Gender, and Class," *Gender and Society* 17, no. 6 (2003), 945.

5. "Number of Comfort Stations and Comfort Women" *Digital Museum, The Comfort Women Issue and the Asian Women's Fund.* https://awf.or.jp/e1/facts-07.html.

families and rejected by their patriarchal communities. Despite the magnitude of human rights violations and victims impacted by this atrocious system of military sexual slavery, the comfort women system was largely overlooked until nearly 50 years after the end of World War II. In 1991, former comfort woman Kim Hak-Sun shared her testimony to the world on a CNN broadcast.[6] Since Kim broke the comfort women story to the general public, Japan and several of the Asian countries from which Japan abducted comfort women have been engaged in constant negotiations centering on proper acknowledgment, apologies, and reparations. This work describes the system of military sexual slavery that Japan worked so hard to erase from historical memory, and it traces Japan's alternating acknowledgment and denial of its comfort women system from the 1990s to the present date.

Chapter I. Historical Background explains how and why comfort stations were created. *Chapter II. The 1990s* describes how the government of Japan initially responded to the breaking of the comfort women story with both denial and apologies, and a refusal to provide adequate reparations. *Chapter III. The 2000s-2010s* describes activists' continued demands for government reparations and the emergence of alternative approaches to seeking justice for former comfort women. The *Conclusion* discusses the government of Japan's contempo-

6. Vicki Sung-Yeon Kwon, "The Sonyŏsang Phenomenon: Nationalism and Feminism Surrounding the 'Comfort Women' Statue." *Korean Studies* 43 (2019), 16.

rary struggles with lingering imperialist and patriarchal attitudes about women's bodies that continue to extend its refusal to take sufficient responsibility for Japan's military sexual slavery. This account not only seeks to spread awareness of the often overlooked atrocities committed in the Pacific Theater during World War II and to demonstrate the need for just and timely reparations but also to highlight how the intersections of factors like imperialism, colonialism, patriarchy, sex, race, ethnicity, nationality, age, and socioeconomic status, all compounded to create the violence and historical erasure that Asian women and girls trapped in military sexual slavery experienced both during their enslavement and for the rest of their lives.

I. Historical Background

Before World War II, Japan had a longstanding culture of legalized prostitution and poor families often sold their daughters into prostitution out of economic necessity. Prostitution and sex in Japan were not regarded with the same moral taboos as it was in Western, Christian-dominated countries. Often, the justification for prostitution in Imperial Japan was that using poor Japanese women to fulfill the needs of the Japanese male population protected the purity of middle and upper-class Japanese women. Middle and upper-class women were to marry, have children for the nation, and act as "Good Wives, Wise Mothers" to raise the nation's next generation.[7] Thus, Japanese citizens' attitudes towards prostitution, sex, and the social roles of Japanese women across classes were deeply intertwined with notions of filial duty and nationalism.

The Imperial Japanese Army (IJA) invaded Manchuria in 1931 with the nationalistic goal of further expanding the empire. Japan sought to bring what it considered its superior language and culture to the rest

---

7. Min, ibid., 952.

of Asia—just as it had previously done in Taiwan and Korea—in a nonconsensual exchange for labor and natural resources. Given Japan's existing practice of prostitution, the creation of a small number of IJA "comfort stations" in the early 1930s in China was not a great leap. The truly dramatic transition from a few comfort stations into a large, military-scale sexual slavery operation occurred shortly after the 1937 Nanjing Massacre. The Nanjing Massacre—or Rape of Nanking—was a period of 6 weeks when Japanese soldiers raped, tortured, and killed hundreds of thousands of Chinese civilians[8] Thereafter, in 1938 Lieutenant-General Okabe Naozaburō issued the following instructions:

> *According to various information, the reason for such strong anti-Japanese sentiment [among the local Chinese population] is widespread rape committed by Japanese military personnel in many places. It is said that such rape is fermenting unexpectedly serious anti-Japanese sentiment... Therefore, the frequent occurrence of rape in various places is not just a matter of criminal law. It is nothing but high treason that breaches public peace and order, that harms the strategic activities of our entire forces, and that brings serious trouble to our nation... It is necessary to eradicate such acts. Any commander who tolerates rape must be condemned as a disloyal subject...*

---

8. Iris Chang, *The Rape of Nanking: The Forgotten Holocaust of World War II*, Basic Books, 1991, 4-6.

> *Therefore it is of vital importance that individ-*
> *ual acts by our military personnel be strictly con-*
> *trolled, and that, at the same time, facilities for*
> *sexual pleasure be established promptly, in order*
> *to prevent our men from inadvertently breaking*
> *the law due to the lack of such facilities.*[9]

Okabe's instruction is not only one of the few pieces of surviving evidence that proves the comfort system was military-organized but reveals much about Japanese soldiers' attitudes about rape. It shows the IJA was surprised that raping Chinese citizens caused "unexpectedly serious anti-Japanese sentiment." It demonstrates that IJA officers were motivated to stop rape for the purposes of military strategy, as opposed to attempting to stop a human rights violation. Okabe's phrasing "inadvertently breaking the law due to the lack of such facilities" reveals the lack of responsibility placed on Japanese soldiers and shows that the IJA did not see rape as something to be stopped, so much as something to be redirected to more discrete and regulated quarters.

The IJA's comfort women system of military sexual slavery was designed with the intent of controlling its soldiers' sexual activity. The "comfort stations" were allegedly designed to simultaneously protect the moral reputation of the IJA, minimize anger from civilians in occupied territories, and prevent troops from contract-

---

9. Tanaka, ibid., 16.

ing venereal disease.[10] Initially, prostitutes were recruited from Japan, but when there proved to be too few, the army switched primarily to coercively taking poor Korean girls from the countryside to keep up with demand. The IJA deliberately sought young, unmarried Korean girls because it was assumed they were less likely to have VD.[11] Some Japanese women who were not prostitutes were also coercively taken, although the IJA preferred Koreans because it was considered bad for Japanese morale if people saw their country's women in comfort stations. The IJA's reluctance to forcibly recruit Japanese women who were not already prostitutes demonstrated the cognitive dissonance military officials may have experienced about claiming that this sexual slavery was "work" and that the conditions of comfort stations were reasonable.

The implementation of the comfort women system did not, however, prevent Japanese soldiers from raping civilians or considerably reduce the spread of VD among troops.[12] While the weekly medical examinations of comfort women for VD and the distribution of condoms

---

10. Tanaka, ibid., 3. There were also many superstitions that justified sex as a military necessity. In George Hick's *The Comfort Women*, Hicks describes the superstitions and beliefs that included, but are not limited to: the superstition that having sex with a virgin before battle protected a soldier from harm, the belief that young men drafted into the army should have sex at least once before dying, the belief that it was necessary for pilots to have sex to improve concentration, the belief that sex "aroused aggression" before battle, and the belief that comfort stations had positive effects on the psyche of soldiers who were away from home for interminable lengths.

11. Tanaka, ibid., 30.

12. Ibid., 28.

to soldiers suggest that the IJA was genuinely concerned about reducing the spread of VD, many of its other justifications for comfort stations fall short. Since local women were often coercively taken and put into comfort stations in their home regions, the stations did not succeed in reducing rape among civilians from occupied territories. Depending on the generals' leniency—and sometimes as a result of direct orders from their generals—many Japanese soldiers deliberately used rape as a form of intimidation and the demasculinization of civilians in occupied regions to weaken morale and resistance. The IJA did not consider preventing its soldiers from raping Chinese civilians by increasing punitive measures and convictions for rapists. The IJA found the following number of soldiers guilty of the combined crime of looting, rape, and manslaughter: 15 men in 1939, 4 men in 1940, and a grand total of two men in 1942.[13] Yuki Tanaka notes that "This Japanese official military data looks absurd when it is compared with the actual evidence, such as various testimonies presented at the Tokyo War Crimes Tribunal regarding the Rape of Nanjing."[14] If the IJA were to actually punish every one of its soldiers who committed crimes against Chinese civilians, it would lose immense numbers of soldiers for fighting.

Japanese soldiers did not see the comfort women system as systematic rape but as a system of prostitution and referred to comfort women as prostitutes. This was because soldiers paid for tickets in exchange for "using"

---

13. Ibid., 29.
14. Ibid.

comfort stations.[15] The cost of using comfort stations depended both on the rank of the soldier and the race of the comfort woman. Enlisted men paid 1.5 or 2 yen out of their 6-10 yen monthly salary to use a comfort station.[16] Higher-ranking officers had to pay more but were eligible for preferred hours and longer durations.[17] The services of Japanese women were more expensive than that of Korean women and the services of Korean women were more expensive than that of Chinese women, demonstrating the colonial and hierarchical nature of Imperial Japan.[18] However, the soldiers' money that was theoretically supposed to pay comfort women for their services was almost always taken by comfort station managers.[19] The few comfort women who received meager payments—comfort women station protocol and conditions ranged dramatically—often earned them in military scrip that became worthless once the war ended.[20] Thus this system was not prostitution because prostitution refers to sex in exchange for money. Furthermore, unlike licensed prostitutes in Japan, comfort women were taken coercively, not allowed to refuse "clients," forced to have sex under the constant threat of violence by men armed with military weapons, and kept imprisoned against their will by military personnel in war zones.

---

15. Ibid., 55.

16. Ibid., 54.

17. George Hicks, et. al., "The Comfort Women," *The Japanese Wartime Empire, 1931-1945*. Princeton University Press, 1996, 317.

18. Ibid., 318.

19. Ibid.

20. Tanaka, ibid., 56.

Underlying the existence of so many different, sometimes contradictory, "practical" and superstitious justifications for the creation of comfort stations, there is the simple truth was that the Imperial Japanese Army wanted to have comfort stations and would say whatever was necessary to legitimize rape and get its request for comfort stations granted. By taking the IJA's practical justifications at face value, several past historians have failed to address that in Japan's colonial and patriarchal society, these men felt entitled to sex. As former comfort woman, Ahn Jeom-sun explained "What can I say? They did all the stuff that they wanted to do according to their desires, or according to what they wanted. This was all forced. What could we possibly do?"[21]

Cover-Up

Although the IJA felt entitled to comfort stations, officers were aware of how people in other nations would negatively view military sexual slavery and worked to keep comfort women secret both during and after the war. One document prepared by the Ministry of War is an instruction entitled 'Matters related to the recruitment of female and other employees for military comfort stations,' which was issued on March 4, 1938 to the

---

21. Elise Hu, "'Comfort Woman' Memorial Statues, a Thorn in Japan's Side, Now Sit on Korean Buses." *NPR*, 13 Nov. 2017, https://www.npr.org/sections/parallels/2017/11/13/563838610/comfort-woman-memorial-statues-a-thorn-in-japans-side-now-sit-on-korean-buses.

Chiefs of Staff of the North China Area Army and Central China Area Army. It states:

> In recruiting female and other employees from Japan for the establishment of comfort stations in the place where the China Incident occurred, some deliberately make an illicit claim that they have permissions from the military authorities, thus damaging the Army's reputation and causing misunderstanding among the general population... Due to the selection of unsuitable recruiting agents, some have been arrested and investigated by the police because of their [dubious] methods of recruitment and kidnapping... In actual recruitment, each Army must work in close cooperation with local Kempeitai or police authorities, thus maintaining the Army's dignity and avoiding social problems.[22]

This illuminating 1938 Ministry of War document is not only a key piece of evidence that shows the IJA coercively recruited women into sexual slavery with the help of recruiters, the Kempeitati (IJA secret police) and local police in occupied territories, but it also shows the lengths that the IJA went to hide its involvement. The statement that some recruiters made that they were backed by the authority of the IJA was truthful and therefore "illicit" because it threatened the IJA's reputation and caused resentment among civilians. Despite

---

22. Tanaka, ibid., 23.

Japan's efforts, people from its occupied territories noticed when beautiful, young women and girls were being forcibly taken by military men in large numbers. Thus, the question of secrecy was less about genuinely deceiving local populaces and more about covering overt links to the military and repressing allegations against the IJA and the Imperial Japanese government. Similarly, other nations such as the U.S. knew about the secret of comfort women[23] but had other war priorities.

U.S. Army. *Comfort women (comfort girls) captured by U.S. Army, August 14 1944, Myitkyina*, August 14 1944.[24]

---

23. For instance, a famous comfort women photograph shows captured Korean comfort women being interrogated by Japanese-American soldiers in August 1944 (Tanaka, ibid., 41).

24. Photograph. Photograph from U.S. National Archives. Source: WikimediaCommons,https://commons.wikimedia.org/w/index.php?title=File:Captured_comfort_women_in_Myitkyina_on_August_14_in_1944.jpg.

The ambiguity that denial and censorship create acts as a veil and allows perpetrators to commit greater atrocities and for bystanders to remain complicit. In the last days of World War II, the IJA would kill comfort women, abandon comfort women, and sometimes even dress comfort women as nurses and deposit them in hospitals so that Allied powers would not see the incriminating evidence linking the IJA to comfort stations.[25] Upon defeat, the IJA and the government of Japan immediately destroyed most of its military documents that contained proof of war crimes, including the comfort women system.[26] The IJA did not feel the need to systematically hunt down and kill all former comfort women who were dispersed in foreign countries, probably because it could count on the language barriers, immense stigma, shame, and the low social standing that comfort women experienced as victims of sexual violence in patriarchal societies to keep them from reporting their horrific abuse.

---

25. George Hicks, *The Comfort Women*. W. W. Norton & Company, Inc., 1997, 154-155, 157.
26. Hicks, ibid., 306.

II. The 1990s

The Comfort Women Story Comes to Light

Although the United States knew about comfort women —from U.S. soldiers encountering comfort women during the war in the Pacific Theater and throughout the U.S. Occupation of Japan—the U.S. chose not to prosecute many of Japan's war crimes in order to facilitate a peaceful post-war transition and build up Japan as a democratic country to counter communist countries in Asia. U.S. officers in Tokyo chose only to prosecute what *they* deemed were the most serious crimes convicted by the most serious perpetrators (with the notable exception of Emperor Hirohito) and did not rank rape highly on the list of war crimes. Furthermore, some historians have argued that the U.S.'s failure to prosecute the comfort system was because U.S. soldiers themselves used both comfort stations and brothels in Japan during the U.S. occupation.[27]

---

27. Tanaka, ibid., 2.

Yokosuka City Council, "Yasuura House (Recreation and
Amusement Association," 1945-46.[28]

Between 1945-1991, the comfort women story was
investigated by some journalists, scholars, and activists,
and quietly remained under the surface in public memory in Korea. When South Korea became a democracy in
1987, citizens were able to discuss the plight of comfort
women in earnest.[29] In 1990, Professors Yun Chung-ok
and Lee Hyo-Chae worked with women's organizations
to found the Korean Council for the Women Drafted for
Military Sexual Slavery by Japan or "The Korean Coun-

28. Photograph. Source: Wikimedia Commons.
    https://commons.wikimedia.org/w/index.php?title=File:Yasuura_
    House.jpg.
29. "How did the Comfort Women Issue come to light?" *Digital Museum:
    The Comfort Women Issue and the Asian Women's Fund.* Accessed 7
    July 2022. https://www.awf.or.jp/e2/survey.html.

cil" for short.[30] That same year, a government official made a statement that both denied the Japanese government's orchestration of the comfort system and posited that an investigation of the comfort system would be fruitless.[31] For decades the comfort women story had always been there, and there were organizations like the Korean Council protesting, however, the story finally broke globally on August 14, 1991, when 67-year-old Kim Hak-Sun testified about her experience as a former comfort woman.[32]

While many former comfort women stayed silent due to the fear of bringing shame to their families, once Kim's husband and children died, she felt that she could share her story. Her testimony inspired other comfort women to share their testimonies, and scholars and activists continued to raise further awareness. On January 11, 1992, the *Asahi* newspaper published Japanese Professor Yoshimi Yoshiaki's recently discovered government documents implicating the Japanese government's role as the orchestrators of the comfort women system.[33] Although Kim Hak-Sun's testimony was made several months prior, it is likely that the authority of a male, Japanese professional citing written evidence over oral testimony, was received more seriously by male Japanese government officials in patriarchal Japan. The crucial combination of the firsthand testimony of women

---

30. Soh, ibid., 1232-1233.
31. "How did the Comfort Women Issue come to light?", ibid.
32. Kwon, ibid., 16.
33. George Hicks et al., "The 'Comfort Women,'" ibid., 308; Sarah C. Soh, ibid., 209.

who were sexually enslaved, uncovered documentary evidence, and the increasingly liberal and globalized conditions of the 1990s catapulted the long-hidden story of comfort women—and Japan along with it—into the international spotlight.

Government of Japan's Response

On January 1, 1992, Prime Minister Kiichi Miyazawa apologized in a press conference and on January 17, 1992—five months after Kim Hak-Sun's testimony and several days after the release of Professor Yoshimi's findings—he issued an apology during his visit to South Korea's capital, Seoul, and Japan began an internal investigation into the comfort system.[34] Although the long-awaited formal recognition and apology made groundbreaking progress, there proved to be a big difference between Japan's willingness to acknowledge a comfort system existed and Japan's willingness to accept the horrific facts of the comfort system and hold itself morally and legally accountable.

The Japanese government's initial framing of the comfort system falsely portrayed it as privately-operated, voluntary prostitution, as opposed to military-organized, coerced sexual slavery.[35] The government of Japan repeatedly emphasized that it was often private recruiters who "recruited" comfort women, while point-

---

34. Hicks, ibid., 308.
35. Ibid., 307.

edly ignoring that these recruiters were hired by lower military officers who were ordered to gather quotas of comfort women by high-ranking military officers. The Japanese government also frequently fell back on the argument that there is not sufficient documentary evidence to support the claims that comfort women were forcibly taken while omitting the 1945 Japanese government's role in destroying the relevant documents. The emphasis on documentary evidence reinforced the colonialist view of valuing written sources over oral history. The government of Japan's stance on written evidence sought to minimize the validity of the numerous verbal testimonies of surviving comfort women, alongside the physical proof on their bodies in the form of scars and medical complications.

On August 4, 1993, the government of Japan released the famous Kono Statement, summarizing the government's investigations into the comfort women system and the government's first official acknowledgment that the military had *some* involvement and that *some* comfort women were recruited through coercive means.[36] Since the release of the Kono Statement, many Japanese politicians have denied its accuracy, while South Korean citizens have protested its misleading understatements and demanded a complete, revised statement.

---

36. Ji Young Kim, and Jeyong Sohn, "Settlement Without Consensus: International Pressure, Domestic Backlash, and the Comfort Women Issue in Japan." *Pacific Affairs* 90, no. 1, 2017, 84.

Seeking Reparations

Although each survivor had her own conception of justice, a few consistent demands emerged. Overwhelmingly, former comfort women wanted the government of Japan to "(i) acknowledge that the comfort women were forcibly taken away; (ii) issue a public apology; (iii) conduct an investigation to discover what really happened and disclose the findings; (iv) construct a monument to commemorate the victims; (v) pay compensation to the victims or their surviving heirs; and (vi) establish educational programs to raise awareness of the history behind the issue."[37] The variety of reparations demanded by former comfort women demonstrates the complexity of delivering justice for survivors and contradicts the claims made by conservative Japanese critics that former comfort women sought free money. It was extremely important to former comfort women to have the violence they suffered acknowledged and taught to subsequent generations. They demanded economic reparations from the government of Japan not only to help them survive in their remaining years but because economic reparations from the government would be a tangible, legitimizing statement that government-sponsored crimes had been committed against them.

The legitimizing implications of the government paying economic reparations to victims were not lost on the government of Japan and thus it fervently resisted. The government of Japan claimed that it was not legally

---

37. "How did the Comfort Women Issue come to light?", ibid.

responsible for paying reparations to comfort women through a variety of arguments that included references to the 1951 San Francisco Peace Treaty and the Japan-Korea 1965 Basic Relations Treaty.[38] In the 1951 treaty, Japan agreed to uphold the sentences of the Tokyo War Crimes trials in Article 11 and agreed to pay reparations to the Allied Powers in Article 14.[39] However, the Tokyo War Crimes Trials themselves failed to address both colonialism and sexual violence.[40] Since the overwhelming majority of comfort women were taken from Korea, Japan also emphasized its payment of war reparations by citing Japan and Korea's 1965 Basic Relations Treaty, in which Japan paid Korea a one-time payment of $300,000,000 in aid and $200,000,000 in low-interest loans for its colonization of Korea from 1910-1945.[41] The Basic Relations Treaty was intended to address the eco-

38. "Establishment of the AW Fund, and the basic nature of its projects." *Digital Museum: The Comfort Women Issue and the Asian Women's Fund*. Accessed 7 July 2022. https://awf.or.jp/e2/foundation.html.
39. "No. 1832 ARGENTINA, AUSTRALIA, BELGIUM, BOLIVIA, BRAZIL, etc. Treaty of Peace with Japan (with two declarations). Signed at San Francisco, on 8 September 1951" 14 June. 2022. https://treaties.un.org/doc/publication/unts/volume%20136/volume-136-i-1832-english.pdf, 56, 60.
40. Elizabeth W. Son, "Staging Justice: The Women's International War Crimes Tribunal." In *Embodied Reckonings: "Comfort Women," Performance, and Transpacific Redress*, 65-102. University of Michigan Press, 2018, 73.
41. Hicks, ibid., 308; "No. 8473 Japan and Republic of Korea Agreement on the settlement of problems concerning property and claims and on economic co-operation (with Protocols, exchanges of notes and agreed minutes). Signed at Tokyo, on 22 June 1965" 10 June. 2022. https://treaties.un.org/doc/Publication/UNTS/Volume%20583/volume-583-I-8473-English.pdf, 258.

nomic deprivation Korea suffered as Japan gained wealth by exploiting Korea and to pave the way for future mutually beneficial trade between the two countries. Opponents of these arguments have countered that neither treaty explicitly addressed the comfort system (whose existence was known to few at the time of these treaties' signings) and that the Basic Relations Treaty in particular was primarily intended to be an economic treaty, not a hall pass for crimes against humanity. Furthermore, the disregard for the inclusion of women and girls in considerations for war crime trials in the 1950s and 1960s should not preclude women and girls from belatedly getting justice and reparations once the world finally recognized the validity of the violence committed against them as having the status of war crimes in the 1990s.

The Government of Japan and Japanese courts also cited sovereign immunity and Japan's civil statute of limitations, the latter, which Gay Johnson McDougall explains in a 1998 UN report, does not apply to international law regarding war crimes and crimes against humanity. Japan's repeated argument that it had previously settled World War II crimes multiple times in multiple treaties demonstrated its fear that in acknowledging comfort women, it would be caught in a never-ending series of reparations for its older generations' actions. South Korea's repeated argument that military sexual slavery (and many other colonial atrocities) were not addressed in those previous treaties, demonstrated its fear that history would continue to be forgotten and thus wrongs against Korean people would continue to occur.

Protests, Publications, and Press

Claire Solery, "Comfort Women, rally in front of the Japanese Embassy in Seoul, August 2011".[42]

In 1992, former comfort women began holding weekly protests at noon called "Wednesday Demonstrations" outside the Japanese embassy in South Korea. They made themselves visible and spoke out to the South Korean public. Soon, the South Korean public—particularly students—joined in. Through the help of non-governmen-

---

42. Photograph. Source: Wikimedia Commons, https://commons.wikimedia.org/w/index.php?title=File:Comfort_Women,_rally_in_front_of_the_Japanese_Embassy_in_Seoul,_August_2011_(3).jpg.

tal organizations (NGOs), comfort women also began publishing their stories. In 1995, the Korean Council for Women Drafted for Military Sexual Slavery by Japan (the Council) published a book of testimonies from formerly enslaved women who were interviewed, including Kim Hak-Sun. This publication gave women a platform to tell their story and their firsthand accounts gave a more complete understanding of Japan's military sexual slavery.

In Kim Hak-Sun's chapter "Bitter Memories I am Loath to Recall," she describes her childhood before the war when she was forcibly taken by soldiers at the age of 17 to comfort stations. Kim describes how she and other Korean girls were given to the Japanese at comfort stations. Kim describes her loss of virginity by being raped, and many subsequent rapes, as well as beatings if she refused soldiers' demands. Kim states that she "never received any money all the time I was a comfort woman" and tells of the abuse she suffered by her husband for her past as a comfort woman, and explains how as an old woman "I feel I could tear apart, limb by limb, those who took away my innocence and made me as I am."[43] By being given the freedom to shape her own narrative, Kim began her testimony by describing her childhood and the person she was before her liberty was taken. She was also able to emphasize how her experience in sexual slavery impacted her for the remainder of her life, demonstrating how the suffering she experienced was neither confined to acts of sexual violence nor the perpetrators

---

43. Hak-Sun Kim, "Bitter Memories I am Loath to Recall." *True Stories of the Korean Comfort Women*, edited by Keith Howard, Cassell, 1995, 37.

of those acts of sexual violence. Much of the suffering that survivors of sexual slavery experienced was isolation after rejection from society. In sharing their stories, former comfort women were not only telling the world what happened so as to prevent sexual slavery from occurring again, but they implicitly and explicitly argued that patriarchal norms also inflicted violence and would also need to be changed to prevent the same suffering for future victims of institutionalized sexual violence.

Kim's testimony also has many political implications. Her description of how Korean girls were forced to assume Japanese names and clothing, and how women who spoke Japanese fared slightly better under the comfort system demonstrates the colonial nature of this system of sexual slavery. Through both forced assimilation and forced sexual slavery, women were denied not only their bodily autonomy but their identities too. After the war, their status as former comfort women has continued to obscure other aspects of their identity. Kim's statements about how soldiers forcibly recruited her, the soldiers' raping her and taking her virginity, and the statement that she never received money for her "work" in comfort stations, all contradicted the Japanese government's narrative of "voluntary prostitution." Although feminist movements and political reforms in Asia made the 1990s' political climate more viable for Asian women to discuss sexual violence, former comfort women faced doubt and backlash from the general public.

A 1992 article in *The Economist* covering Filipina former comfort women speaking out mostly discussed the Philippines' embarrassment of attention being drawn to its sex industry.[44] Rather than quote the protesting former comfort women, the article opted to quote a male columnist from a Manila newspaper who said that "because of the hard times in wartime Manila, he says, many women volunteered to serve in Japanese brothels. 'Quite a number of Philippine women developed relations with Japanese officers and were proud of it.' He concluded, 'A national shame is best kept in a tight closet.'"[45] The emphasis on national pride over the violation of women's human rights was a recurring theme in the discussion of comfort women. In its subsequent issue, *The Economist* published a letter to the editor by a Filipina woman living in California named Corazon Cole who angrily clarified:

> *"A great number of women were raped, tortured, and killed by the Japanese during their occupation of the Philippines. Any portrayal of Philippine women as mere tramps of the world is a gross injustice."*[46]

Interestingly, Cole cited her education and Catholicism to argue that "There are millions of women in the Phil-

44. "Problem of the comfort women." *Economist*, October 31, 1992, 76+. *The Economist Historical Archive* (accessed August 5, 2022). https://link-gale-com.ezproxy.whitman.edu/apps/doc/GP4100240987/ECON?u=whitman&sid=bookmark-ECON&xid=da66e53d.

45. Ibid.

46. Cole Corazon, "Japan in the war." Economist, 26 Dec. 1992, p. 8. The Economist Historical Archive. http://link.gale.com/apps/doc/GP4100242386/ECON?u=whitman&sid=bookmark-ECON&xid=203848a6. Accessed 5 June 2022.

ippines who are as educated and respectable as I am," demonstrating how women had to prove themselves to be Madonnas within the patriarchal Madonna-whore complex to assert they should be respected.[47] This limiting pure-corrupt dichotomy often reinforced patriarchal norms and left little room for Asian women who were "corrupted" against their will to reintegrate into society.

Establishment of the AWF

In 1995 the Japanese government created the Asian Women's Fund (AWF). The humanitarian fund functioned to circumvent Japan's legal culpability while appeasing protestors that demanded reparations. The AWF was funded by a combination of private donations by Japanese citizens and some portion of government funding. Emphasizing that these were humanitarian gifts and not reparations, the AWF promised each verified former comfort woman $20,000, medical payments for complications caused by sexual enslavement, and a written letter of apology from the prime minister. The AWF was designed for former comfort women from South Korea, the Philippines, the Netherlands, Indonesia and Taiwan but excluded other critical nations such as China.[48] The AWF's exclusion of China, despite the large number of

---

47. Ibid.
48. "Measure Taken by the Government of Japan on the Issue of 'comfort women,'" *Ministry of Foreign Affairs of Japan*, 14 January 2021 https://www.mofa.go.jp/policy/women/fund/policy.html.

Chinese comfort women—and the even larger number of Chinese women and girls not trapped in the comfort system who were raped by IJA soldiers throughout the 1930s and 1940s—was a glaring insufficiency that shows the limits of the AWF's work from the outset. The creation of the AWF received a lot of backlash in both Japan and Korea. Most comfort women indignantly refused to be "paid off," and many questioned why the prime minister, and not the emperor, was signing the apology. Many Japanese conservatives questioned why Japan had to pay foreigners at all.

The seven Korean former comfort women that accepted donations from the AWF in 1997 were harassed by women's groups for giving in and not fighting for legal reparations. At the lobbying of The Korean Council for the Women Drafted for Military Sexual Slavery by Japan, the government of Korea created a counter-fund for Korean former comfort women of about $26,000 on the condition that recipients do not accept AWF money and excluded women who accepted AWF money from eligibility.[49] The unwillingness of activists to respect that individual comfort women could make autonomous decisions about whether they would like to receive or refuse reparations from Japan shows once again how the sexual exploitation of women became an issue of national pride and diplomacy that manifested another kind of exploitation of these women.

---

49. Soh, ibid., 228-229.

Legal Accountability: Court Cases and Beyond

Throughout the 1990s, groups of both Korean and Chinese former comfort women filed several class-action lawsuits in Japan against Japan's government. Some of these lawsuits were aided by Japanese lawyers, who upon learning about the comfort women system for the first time, worked pro bono to represent former comfort women who otherwise would not have been able to afford legal representation.[50] The actions of Japanese citizens as early as the 1990s show once again the variations between the government of Japan's response to comfort women and much of the Japanese public's response to comfort women. The aid of organizations and pro bono work was necessary because of the destitution most former comfort women experienced from being displaced, uncompensated for their "work," and often unable to marry after the war, and therefore unable to be supported by a husband in patriarchal countries where there are few economic opportunities for poor women of color. In all cases former comfort women lost and all appeals were rejected by the Supreme Court.[51] The lack of justice was devastating, particularly since the former comfort women sacrificed so much of their privacy to participate in the class action lawsuits. The

---

50. Xiaoyang Hao, "Transmitting Knowledge and Gaining Recognition: Chinese 'Comfort Women' Reparation Trails in the 1990s and 2000s," *The Asia-Pacific Journal*, Volume 19, Issue 5, March 1, 2021, 1.

51. Hao, ibid., 1-2.

small silver lining for the plaintiffs was that even losses brought increased visibility to the comfort women system and provided a platform for their testimonies.

Towards the end of the 1990s' decade of protests and lawsuits, a UN subcommittee published the 1998 report "Contemporary Forms of Slavery: Systematic rape, sexual slavery and slavery-like practices during armed conflict," in which it explicitly defined Japan's acts in creating and perpetuating the comfort woman system as crimes, explained that Japan had a duty to prosecute criminals and provide reparations, and provided recommendations for reparations. Despite some limited international pressure, other nations did not strongly push Japan. Not only was there reluctance to get involved in something that had remained dormant for over 50 years, and to the extent that other countries claim to care about the sexual exploitation of women, many scholars have posited that, in addition to caring less about women's issues in general, western nations cared less about the exploitation of women of color than of white women.

III. The 2000s-2010s

Voice of America, "File: Taipei Women's Rescue Foundation 2013-9,"
September 5, 2013.[52]

The contentious debate over apologies and reparations
for comfort women that began in the 1990s carried

---

52. Photograph. Source: Wikimedia Commons,
https://commons.wikimedia.org/w/index.php?title=File:Taipei_
Women%27s_Rescue_Foundation_2013-9_(1).jpg.

over into the 21st century. After several groups of comfort women's unsuccessful attempts through the Japanese legal system, in September 2000, former comfort women from four nations filed a class-action lawsuit in the U.S., citing its ability to hear international cases because of the Alien Tort Claims Act.[53] Unfortunately, the D.C. Circuit dismissed the case as being outside of its jurisdiction. It became clear that other avenues for redress would need to be taken.

Women's International War Crimes Tribunal

In response to Japan's delay of legal action as it waited for elderly former comfort women to pass away, and the U.S.'s unwillingness to intervene, several organizations from several countries came together to hold The Women's International War Crimes Tribunal in Tokyo from December 8-12 in 2000. In this symbolic hearing, women who were formerly forced into sexual slavery were finally given the time, space, and respect in their final years to share their testimonies before judges and have their experiences validated with the recognition by judicial figures that military sexual slavery and the abuses they suffered under it were in fact crimes. Legal scholar Nicola Henry explains the double bind that victims of sexual violence experience, where trauma is both the requisite for gaining validity as a victim, yet trauma simultaneously lessens the validity of a victim's

53. Son, ibid., 74.

testimony as a reliable witness in the court's eye.[54] The Women's Tribunal created better conditions for women and survivors of sexual violence to share their testimonies than normal courts because the tribunal treated the survivors' testimonies with validity from the outset and because survivors were not constrained by legal etiquette while sharing their testimonies.[55] The tribunal even had former Japanese soldiers testify as key witnesses and describe how they raped women.[56] Thus, the tribunal acted not only as a vehicle for catharsis and justice for victims where conventional legal systems failed, but it also acted as an important tool for preserving the historical memory of the comfort system. Each day of the Tribunal was attended by approximately 600 Japanese citizens, and after the tribunal concluded, its findings were preserved in the newly created Women's Active Museum on War and Peace.[57] To date, WAM is the only museum devoted to the topic of comfort women in Japan.

Educational Curriculum and Textbook Controversies

One of the survivors' demands that the government of Japan resisted, even more greatly than paying reparations (as demonstrated by the creation of the AWF),

---

54. Hao, ibid., 3.
55. For instance, they could gesture in addition to using words to explain what the Japanese soldiers did to them.
56. Son, ibid., 90.
57. Ibid., 81, 100.

was the establishment of educational tools and memorials to remember the atrocities of the comfort women system in the public school curriculum. The brief liberal period when the conservative LDP was not in power (1993-1994) combined with the 50th anniversary of World War II in 1995 created a movement for discussing wartime atrocities. The liberal movement quickly subsided when the LDP regained power and was snubbed by Prime Minister Abe's 2007 Educational reforms.[58] That same year, Prime Minister Abe denied that comfort women were coercively taken.[59] Mid-1990s textbooks had begun adding discussions of comfort women to middle school history textbooks, only to water down or entirely omit them in the 2000s.[60] The rationalization for this erasure was that content about sex and sexual violence was considered inappropriate for middle school students. The solution of deleting history, as opposed to the intuitive solution of moving the content into high school history textbooks, is questionable. Peter Cave notes that the decision to add comfort women (and subsequently remove comfort women) from middle school textbooks was based on the fact that Japan only legally requires 9 years of compulsory education and not all high schools have to

---

58. Adam Lebowitz, and David McNeill, "Hammering Down the Educational Nail: Abe Revises the Fundamental Law of Education," *The Asia-Pacific Journal* Vol. 5, Issue 7, 12 Jul 2007, 1.

59. Hirofumi Hayashi, "Disputes in Japan over the Japanese Military 'Comfort Women' System and Its Perception in History," *The Annals of the American Academy of Political and Social Science* 617 (2008), 1.

60. Kim and Sohn, ibid., 89.

teach Japanese history.[61] However, Cave also notes that 96 percent of children choose to continue their education into high school.[62] It would not be impossible to introduce the subject of comfort women at the middle school level and incorporate the subject of comfort women into high school material in greater depth, just as the holocaust is taught in different degrees of detail adjusted for age in public middle schools and high schools in the United States.

Sonyŏsang Statue outside the Japanese Embassy in Seoul, Korea

Another key demand of many former comfort women was for Japan to erect memorials so that people would not forget about Japan's military sexual slavery. The government of Japan not only resisted memorialization but actively tried to stop other nations from erecting comfort women memorials. A contemporary debate about comfort women between Japan and Korea arose in 2011 when a bronze sculpture of a 13-17-year-old comfort woman was placed outside the Japanese embassy in Seoul to honor the 1,000[th] Wednesday Demonstration.[63] The statue, called *pyonghwaui Sonyŏsang* ("The Statue of a Girl for Peace"), was a great source of humil-

---

61. Peter Cave, "Japanese Colonialism and the Asia-Pacific War in Japan's History Textbooks: Changing Representations and Their Causes." *Modern Asian Studies* 47, no. 2, 2013, 544.

62. Ibid., 544.

63. Kwon, ibid., 7-8.

iation for Japan.[64] In particular, the artists' decision to portray the statue as a young girl who was raped, as opposed to the aged *Halmoni*[65] that protested outside of the embassy, enraged Japanese opponents of the statue, who claimed that comfort women were voluntary prostitutes and not virgin girls forcibly taken from Korea.[66] The Japanese Government demanded that South Korea remove the *Sonyŏsang* statue from the front of the Japanese Embassy. Despite the Japanese Government's willingness to apologize to comfort women, it did not want to be publicly shamed or have tangible reminders of its crimes in the public eye.

The debate over the *Sonyŏsang* statue eventually contributed to the controversial 2015 deal. The governments of Japan and South Korea secretly devised a "final and irreversible" agreement in which the Japanese government would pay "¥1 billion (approx. $8.3 million) for the South Korean Government to establish the Foundation for Reconciliation and Healing. In return, the South Korean Government agreed to 'make an effort' to remove the statue in front of the Japanese embassy in Seoul."[67] Many South Korean citizens were extremely angry because their government had acted unilaterally and many did not want to strike a deal that removed the statue, and in doing so the memory of comfort women too. Furthermore, by Japan granting money

---

64. Ibid.
65. "Halmoni" is the Korean word for grandmother often used to refer to former comfort women.
66. Kwon, ibid., 21-22.
67. Ibid., 8-9.

Maina Kiai, untitled, people gathered around the *Sonyŏsang* statue.[68]

to South Korea to create a fund, the Japanese Government yet again avoided paying reparations directly to victims. This "final agreement" was by no means final. A mere three weeks after the deal was struck, Prime Minister Abe announced that there was no documentary evidence that comfort women were forcibly taken.[69] South Korea was outraged at what it considered

68. Photograph. Source: British Library's Flickr, https://www.flickr.com/photos/mainakiai/24685487756/in/photolist-DBnztS-aam4aE-Dczivo-2iu9acu-2n6rsbf-2jTYq9w-2jTYktV-2jTYjEa-Eyc3Ah-2jTYmhP-2jTYnA5-2nwAcNQ-2jTYoDc-2jTZevM-5nzNRC-2m3.
69. Hosaka Yugi, "Why Did the 2015 Japan-Korea 'Comfort Women' Agreement Fall Apart?" *The Diplomat*, 18 November 2021, https://thediplomat.com/2021/11/why-did-the-2015-japan-korea-comfort-women-agreement-fall-apart/, 3.

a breach of the agreement and continued demanding apologies. Japan, having paid the ¥1 billion, in turn, was angry that South Korea was not maintaining its end of the deal in promptly removing comfort women memorialization and letting the comfort women issue rest. South Koreans continue fighting the deal. As time passes, fewer *Halmoni* remain, and the importance of the *Sonyŏsang* statue and other memorials to keep the memory of comfort women alive only grows.

Japanese Citizens' Activism

The government of Japan's efforts to erase its history of military sexual slavery and evade culpability was not shared by all of its citizens. Although there is often the risk of overemphasizing exceptional cases of resistance among the compliant masses during World War II—Over two-thirds of Japanese military veterans surveyed from 1998-1999 "replied that Japan should neither apologize nor compensate comfort women survivors because they were paid for their services"[70]—it is important to note that in addition to the remarkable Korean activism surrounding the Wednesday demonstrations and the *Sonyŏsang* statue, there have been many Japanese citizens involved in protesting their government's handling of the comfort women issue. From Japanese scholars and journalists such as Suzuûki Yuko and Matsui Yayori sharing the comfort women

70. Soh, ibid., 232.

story to Japanese lawyers representing former sex slaves pro bono to artists such as Yoshiji Watanabe and Kazuko Yokoi with their traveling "Imagine 21" theater company educating people about World War II atrocities through performance, some Japanese citizens have found ways to recognize and engage with Japan's history of military sexual slavery. Although the AWF was controversial, Japanese citizens donated 448 million yen or 5 million USD from 1995-2000.[71] The comfort women debate has raged on for decades in part because of the multiple perspectives held by both Korean and Japanese governments and individual citizens.

---

71. Ibid., 222.

Conclusion

The government of Japan's unwillingness to assume full responsibility, provide legal reparations to former comfort women, and instate educational reforms to include the history of Japanese military sexual slavery, stems in large part from the fact that Japanese society continues to hold onto many of the pre-war imperialistic, conservative attitudes about nationalism, sex, and women's bodies. Although Japan stopped being an empire at the end of World War II, but since the U.S. deliberately did not prosecute Japan for its many war crimes or punish Emperor Hirohito in order to ensure a seamless transition into peacetime, many of the military and government officials of that era continued their work believing that Japan's actions in World War II were not problematic, let alone crimes against humanity. The empire fell but the imperialist attitudes of many of its people did not end. These attitudes could be the topic of a separate book, however, Japan's attitudes about colonialism, sex, and the role of women can be illustrated perhaps most clearly by Japan's famous struggles with its low Total

Fertility Rate (TFR).[72] Japan's 1.36 TFR (well below the replacement rate of 2.1 births to sustain a population) mimics the low fertility rates of many other post-industrialized nations—as nations industrialize and gain wealth they tend to have increased access to contraceptives, increased years of education for girls, and increased participation of women in the workplace, which further fuels economic development because when men and women work there is twice the number of workers than single sex worker economies—apart from other countries such as the United States (with a 1.7 TFR) account for the fewer births by supplementing the population with immigration.

Japanese leaders, however, cling to its imperialistically rooted notion of *Nihonjinron* or Japanese exceptionalism and want Japan to remain a racially homogenous country. The government of Japan's preferred solution is for Japanese women to have more children, demonstrating how Japanese conservatives continue to see women as sexual tools for the nation. Thus, in the 21st century, men are still expected to be the primary breadwinners while women are expected primarily to raise children. Japanese companies make hiring and promotional decisions within this framework. This means that while many Japanese women *do* participate in the workplace, they disproportionately

---

72. Total Fertility Rate refers to the estimated average number of children women in a group or country are expected to have over the course of their lives. If the TFR of a country is 2, it does not mean that every woman in that country has 2 children.

work part-time or in lower positions than their male counterparts do. Japanese leaders may claim to want greater equality in the workplace and representation for women but they have not actually taken the legislative steps to make workplaces viable for working mothers. With fewer opportunities for women to be promoted to leadership positions, Japan continues to be run overwhelmingly by male government officials and continues to be dominated by the Conservative LDP party.

While many people assume that the present is supposed to be more progressive than the past, "the World Economic Forum's Global Gender Gap Report 2021 Ranked Japan 120th out of 156 countries in terms of gender parity, down 40 places compared to its 2006 ranking."[73] What occurred between 2006 and 2021 to explain this decline? The swell of conservatism and reinforcement of gender roles may be traced to Japan's conservative leadership. From 2006-2007 and again from 2012-2020, Japan was run by its longest-ever serving prime minister, Shinzo Abe. Abe, who in 2007 denied that comfort women were coercively taken, created nationalistic educational reforms in the same year, and who was the prime minister during the infamous 2015 Japan-Korea deal that sought to reform Japan but did not prioritize true gender equality. Abe's policies to promote "womenomics" were criticized for being "more about encouraging women back into the workplace to

---

73. Mariko Oi, "Why Japan Can't Shake Sexism," BBC, April 8 2021, https://www.bbc.com/wprklfe/article/20210405-why-japan-cant-shake-sexism.

help the economy, rather than addressing existing challenges such as the lack of childcare to make it easier to juggle work and kids."[74]

Upon Shinzo Abe's tragic assassination on July 8, 2022, when the former prime minister was speaking at a rally in support of an LDP politician, newspapers began to flood with sympathetic portrayals of Abe's attempts to reform Japan. In a Washington Post article titled "What the World Got Wrong About Abe," Gearoid Reidy argued that "Abe sought to draw a line under the awful history of "comfort women"... he wanted Japan to move on, and to have rights that most other countries take for granted—a military with which to defend itself, a country that can be proud of itself despite its brutal and violent past. In any other country, he would likely be an average center-right politician."[75] Reidy quoted Abe speaking at the 70th Anniversary of World War II, whereupon after apologizing, Abe stated Japan "must not let our children, grandchildren, and even further generations to come, who have nothing to do with that war, be predestined to apologize."[76] The issue with this framing, however, is that Japan cannot truly "move on" or "apologize" if it does not first truly engage with its past war atrocities. The notion that current and future generations of Japan "have nothing to do with that war"

---

74. Ibid.
75. Reidy, Gearoid, "What the World Got Wrong About Shinzo Abe," *The Washington Post* July 13 2022, https://www.washingtonpost.com/business/what-the-world-got-wrong-about-shinzo-abe/2022/07/12/2cb5f096-0237-11ed-8beb-2b4e481b1500_story.html.
76. Ibid.

is a falsehood when World War II has shaped so much of the nation that the younger generations have inherited. Japan's modern economic success had the support of 35 years of exploiting Korea as its colony and then another seven years of U.S. occupation in which the U.S. spent a little over 2 billion dollars (15 billion in 2005 dollars) reconstructing Japan. Its culture of pacifism is directly related to its defeat in World War II, the U.S.'s dropping of atomic bombs on its civilians, and the U.S. occupation's banning of a Japanese national army beyond a self-defense force. Japan's culture of how to treat women is also inextricably tied to its history. Until Japan addresses its imperialistic, patriarchal culture, neither Japan nor Korea will find a resolution.

In order to break the cycle of acknowledgment and denial, Japan needs to move the conversation beyond haggling over economic reparations. At this point, there are so few survivors and prior attempts at economic reparations have demonstrated that without sincere apologies and other forms of reparation, survivors feel that the monetary reparations are incomplete. Instead, Japan needs to focus on fixing its largest deficiencies in accepting responsibility for the comfort women system: erecting memorials, adding the full truth of Japan's history of military sexual slavery into Japan's educational curriculum, and addressing how today's Japan views and treats women in the 21st century. Japan is not the only nation, however, that needs to institute changes. While several other nations have erected comfort women memorials, they have largely remained idle bystanders that have allowed Japan to shirk responsibility for decades. To truly create a world that values the human rights of women and girls of color other nations also need to implement reforms.

Works Cited

Bhattacharya, Suryatapa, and Alyssa Lukpat. "Shinzo Abe's Assassination Draws Grief and Shock from World Leaders; Tributes to the Former Japanese Prime Minister Underscored His Impact on the Region." *Wall Street Journal (Online),* July 8 2022, *ProQuest.* Web. July 15 2022.

Cave, Peter. "Japanese Colonialism and the Asia-Pacific War in Japan's History Textbooks: Changing Representations and Their Causes." *Modern Asian Studies* 47, no. 2 (2013): 542-80. http://www.jstor.org/stable/23359830.

Chang, Iris. "Introduction." *The Rape of Nanking: The Forgotten Holocaust of World War II*, Basic Books, 1991, 4-6.

Cole, Corazon. "Japan in the war." Economist, December 26 1992, p. 8. The Economist Historical Archive, Accessed June 5 2022. http://link.gale.com/apps/doc/GP4100242386/ECON?u=whitman&sid=-bookmark-ECON&xid=203848a6.

"Establishment of the AW Fund, and the basic nature of its projects." *Digital Museum: The Comfort Women*

Issue and the Asian Women's Fund. Accessed July 7 2022. https://awf.or.jp/e2/foundation.html.

Hayashi, Hirofumi. "Disputes in Japan over the Japanese Military 'Comfort Women' System and Its Perception in History." *The Annals of the American Academy of Political and Social Science* 617 (2008): 123-32. http://www.jstor.org/stable/25098017.

Hicks, George. *The Comfort Women*. W. W. Norton & Company, Inc., 1997.

Hicks, George, Peter Duus, Ramon H. Myers, Mark R. Peattie, Wan-yao Chou, Carter J. Eckert, L. H. Gann, et al. "The 'Comfort Women.'" In *The Japanese Wartime Empire, 1931-1945*, edited by Peter Duus, Ramon H. Myers, and Mark R. Peattie, 305-23. Princeton University Press, 1996. https://doi.org/10.2307/j.ctv1mjqvc6.14.

Hao, Xiaoyang. "Transmitting Knowledge and Gaining Recognition: Chinese 'Comfort Women' Reparation Trails in the 1990s and 2000s." *The Asia-Pacific Journal*, Volume 19, Issue 5, March 1, 2021.

"How did the Comfort Women Issue come to light?" *Digital Museum: The Comfort Women Issue and the Asian Women's Fund*. Accessed July 7 2022. https://www.awf.or.jp/e2/survey.html.

Hu, Elise. "'Comfort Woman' Memorial Statues, a Thorn in Japan's Side, Now Sit on Korean Buses." *NPR*, NPR, November 13 2017, https://www.npr.org/sections/parallels/2017/11/13/563838610/comfort-woman-memorial-statues-a-thorn-in-japans-side-now-sit-on-korean-buses.

Kim, Hak-Sun. "Bitter Memories I am Loath to Recall." *True Stories of the Korean Comfort Women,* edited by Keith Howard, Cassell, 1995, 32-40.

Kim, Ji Young, and Jeyong Sohn. "Settlement Without Consensus: International Pressure, Domestic Backlash, and the Comfort Women Issue in Japan." *Pacific Affairs* 90, no. 1 (2017): 77-99. http://www.jstor.org/stable/44876137.

Kwon, Vicki Sung-yeon. "The Sonyŏsang Phenomenon: Nationalism and Feminism Surrounding the 'Comfort Women' Statue." *Korean Studies* 43 (2019): 6-39. doi:10.1353/ks.2019.0006.

Lebowitz, Adam, and David McNeill. "Hammering Down the Educational Nail: Abe Revises the Fundamental Law of Education," *The Asia-Pacific Journal* Vol. 5, Issue 7 (July 12 2007).

"Measure Taken by the Government of Japan on the Issue of 'comfort women'" *Ministry of Foreign Affairs of Japan.* January 14, 2021. https://www.mofa.go.jp/policy/women/fund/policy.html.

Min, Pyong Gap. "Korean 'Comfort Women': The Intersection of Colonial Power, Gender, and Class." *Gender and Society* 17, no. 6 (2003): 938-57. http://www.jstor.org/stable/3594678.

"No. 1832 ARGENTINA, AUSTRALIA, BELGIUM, BOLIVIA, BRAZIL, etc. Treaty of Peace with Japan (with two declarations). Signed in San Francisco on September 8 1951" 14 June. 2022. https://treaties.un.org/doc/publication/unts/volume%20136/volume-136-i-1832-english.pdf.

"No. 8473 Japan and Republic of Korea Agreement on the settlement of problems concerning property and claims and on economic co-operation (with Protocols, exchanges of notes and agreed minutes). Signed in Tokyo on June 22 1965" June 10. 2022. https://treaties.un.org/doc/Publication/UNTS/Volume%20583/volume-583-I-8473-English.pdf.

"Number of Comfort Stations and Comfort Women" *Digital Museum The Comfort Women Issue and the Asian Women's Fund.* https://awf.or.jp/e1/facts-07.html.

Oi, Mariko. "Why Japan Can't Shake Sexism," BBC, April 8 2021, https://www.bbc.com/wprklfe/article/20210405-why-japan-cant-shake-sexism.

"Problem of the comfort women." *Economist*, October 31, 1992, 76+. *The Economist Historical Archive* (accessed August 5, 2022). https://link-gale-com.ezproxy.whitman.edu/apps/doc/GP4100240987/ECON?u=whitman&sid=-bookmark-ECON&xid=da66e53d.

Reidy, Gearoid. "What the World Got Wrong About Shinzo Abe." *The Washington Post* July 13 2022, https://www.washingtonpost.com/business/what-the-world-got-wrong-about-shinzo-abe/2022/07/12/2cb5f096-0237-11ed-8beb-2b4e481b1500_story.html.

Rich, Motoko, Makiko Inoue, Hikari Hida, and Hisako Ueno. "Shinzo Abe is Assassinated with a Homemade Gun, Shocking a Nation." *New York Times*, July 8, 2022, Late Edition (East Coast). http://ezproxy.whitman.edu/login.

Soh, C. Sarah. "Japan's National/Asian Women's Fund for 'Comfort Women.'" *Pacific Affairs* 76, no. 2 (2003): 209-33. http://www.jstor.org/stable/40024391.

Soh, Chunghee Sarah. "The Korean 'Comfort Wom-en': Movement for Redress." *Asian Survey* 36, no. 12 (1996): 1226-40. https://doi.org/10.2307/2645577.

Son, Elizabeth W. "Staging Justice: The Women's International War Crimes Tribunal." In *Embodied Reckonings: "Comfort Women," Performance, and Transpacific Redress*, 65-102. University of Michigan Press, 2018. http://www.jstor.org/stable/10.3998/mpub.8773540.7.

Tanaka, Yuki. *Japan's Comfort Women: Sexual Slavery and Prostitution During World War II and the US Occupation*. London: Taylor & Francis Group, 2001. Accessed August 5, 2022. ProQuest Ebook Central.

Yugi, Hosaka. "Why Did the 2015 Japan-Korea 'Comfort Women' Agreement Fall Apart?" The Diplomat. November 18 2021. https://thediplomat.com/2021/11/why-did-the-2015-japan-korea-comfort-women-agreement-fall-apart/.

Made in the USA
Middletown, DE
26 July 2023